Grammar Book

Chris Speck

Contents

1 How many apples do we need?

1 Read the dialog. What are Elena and her mom doing?

Elena: What do we need to buy for my birthday party tomorrow, Mom?

Mom: Let's look in the fridge.

Elena: How much salad do we want?

Mom: We don't have much salad so we need one bag.

Elena: How many pizzas can we have?

Mom: Well, you have three friends coming to your party. Let's get three pizzas!

Elena: How much fruit do we need?

Mom: We don't need fruit. We have three bananas, two apples, four oranges, and a pear. We have a lot of fruit.

Elena: How many doughnuts should we get?

Mom: Let's get one each!

Elena: So, four? One for each of us at the party?

Mom: No, five. I want one, too!

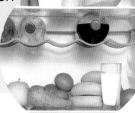

2 Read and answer the questions.

1 How many friends are going to Elena's party? ....

2 How much salad do they need?

    ....

3 How many apples do they have?

    ....

4 How many doughnuts do they need? ....

5 How much fruit do they need?

    ....

3 Read the dialog again and underline *much*, *many*, and *a lot of*.

4 Circle the correct answer.

1 How *much / many* pears do you have in the fridge?

2 We don't have *much / many* eggs in the fridge.

3 I don't like *much / many* salt on my food.

4 I have *a lot of / many* fruit in my lunchbox.

5 How *much / many* fruit do you eat every day?

6 How *much / many* burgers did you eat for dinner?

Grammar

Countable nouns	Uncountable nouns
apples	chocolate
vegetables	sugar
pizzas	rice
burgers	fruit
doughnuts	water
eggs	pasta
How many apples do we need?	How much sugar do we need?
We don't need many apples.	We don't need much sugar.
We need a lot of apples.	We need a lot of sugar.

5 Read the sentences and complete the rules with *much*, *many*, or *a lot of*.

1 How many apples do you want?

2 How much chocolate can I have?

3 We don't have many bananas.

4 There isn't much chocolate.

5 We have a lot of fruit.

6 I like to eat a lot of eggs.

We use .... with countable nouns in negative sentences and questions.

We use .... with countable and uncountable nouns in positive sentences.

We use .... with uncountable nouns in negative sentences and questions.

6 Complete the sentences.

> much (×2)   How much
> How many (×2)   many
> a lot of (×2)

1 I didn't drink .... water yesterday.

2 .... eggs do you have for breakfast?

3 I want .... carrots, I love carrots!

4 .... sugar do you eat every day?

5 Do you like .... salt on your food?

6 I don't eat .... doughnuts.

7 .... people are coming to your birthday party?

8 I need .... bananas. I'm making banana bread.

7 It's your birthday tomorrow. Write a list of all the food you need for your party. Then ask and answer with a friend.

3 pizzas

How many pizzas do you need?

I need three pizzas

How much soda do you need?

I need...

He doesn't drink enough water

1 **Read the text. What kind of food do Tom and Alexa eat?**

I'm Alexa. My brother, Tom, and I love running. We're long distance runners. We like to eat enough good food to stay healthy because we need to run for a long time.

Tom eats a lot of protein and gets it from food like chicken. He needs a lot of carbohydrates so he eats pasta or potatoes with every meal. He says he doesn't eat enough chocolate or enough pancakes!

My favorite meal is fish and rice. It's full of protein, which makes my muscles strong. Tom says I drink too much water, but I think that he doesn't drink enough. I love eating fruit and vegetables. I also make sure I don't eat too many cookies.

Some people eat too much bad food. They eat too many burgers and have soda with too much sugar in it. We like those things too, but only sometimes!

2 **Read and circle T (*true*) or F (*false*).**

1 Alexa enjoys eating vegetables. T / F

2 Alexa likes fish and rice. T / F

3 They eat too many burgers. T / F

4 Tom eats a lot of carbohydrates. T / F

5 Tom thinks he eats enough chocolate. T / F

Grammar

Tom says I drink too much water.

Some people eat too many burgers.

He doesn't eat enough protein.

I eat enough carbohydrates.

3 **Read the text again and underline sentences with *too much*, *too many*, and *enough*.**

4 **Circle the correct answer.**

1 We drink *too much / too many / enough* soda.

2 I think you eat *too much / too many / enough* sugar.

3 I don't drink *too much / too many / enough* water when I run.

4 Some people eat *too much / too many / enough* chocolate bars.

5 Runners need to eat *too much / too many / enough* carbohydrates.

6 It's unhealthy to eat *too much / too many / enough* burgers.

5 Match the sentences to the explanations.

1   I drink too much coffee.
2   I don't drink enough water.
3   I eat too many doughnuts.
4   I eat enough vegetables.

A   I should drink more!
B   I should drink less!
C   I eat the right amount!
D   I should eat fewer!

6 Underline the mistakes and correct the sentences.

1   My uncle eats too much doughnuts. He loves them!

    ....
    ....

2   Pierre is always thirsty because he doesn't drink too many water in the daytime.

    ....
    ....

3   My neighbor eats too much burgers and doesn't do enough exercise.

    ....
    ....

4   Some children drink enough soda.

    ....
    ....

5   Eve doesn't eat too many fruit and vegetables. She should eat more.

    ....
    ....

6   I love chocolate. I eat too many of it.

    ....
    ....

7 Think of the food you ate yesterday. Was it healthy? Ask and answer questions with a friend using *too many*, *too much*, and *enough*.

What did you eat for breakfast?

I ate some bread. I think I had too much butter on my toast!

What did you eat for lunch?

I had chicken and rice, but I didn't eat enough fruit. What about you?

I didn't drink enough water and...

3 I'll have the sushi

1 **Read the dialog. What did Feng decide to order?**

I'm with my dad. I'm at a Japanese restaurant for the first time! It's very exciting and the food is very different. We are really hungry.

Dad: What will you have to eat?

Feng: I don't know. Let me look at the menu.

Dad: I'll have the sushi, I think. I love Japanese food.

Feng: I won't have sushi. Can I have a sandwich?

Dad: No! We're in a Japanese restaurant. You can have sushi, noodles, or tofu. You can have chili chicken soup! They'll bring you anything from the menu.

Feng: I'll just have something simple, like fish sticks.

Dad: They don't have fish sticks!

Feng: OK. I'll have the noodles. Maybe I'll try the sushi next time!

Dad: What would you like to drink?

Feng: I'll have some lemonade, please.

Dad: Will you use the chopsticks?

Feng: I'll try!

2 **Read and write *Yes* or *No*.**

1 Feng won't have the sushi. ....

2 Dad likes Japanese food. ....

3 Feng won't try to use chopsticks. ....

4 Dad will have the steak. ....

5 Feng would like fish sticks. ....

3 **Read again and underline sentences with *will* and *won't*.**

4 **Circle the correct answer.**

Grammar

I/You/He/She/It will have the sushi.	I/You/He/She/It won't have the sushi.
We/You/They will have fish sticks.	We/You/They won't have fish sticks.
will = 'll	will not = won't
Will you try to use the chopsticks?	Yes, I will. No, I won't.

1 What *will / we'll* you have to eat in the restaurant?

2 I think *I'll not / I won't* have the chicken soup for dinner.

3 What *will you / won't you* have to drink?

4 *We'll / We won't* have some noodles because we love them!

5 We *will / won't* eat in the restaurant today. We'll eat at home.

6 Will she use the fork? *Yes, she won't. / Yes, she will.*

5 💡 What's different about these sentences?

1 I often have a glass of milk with my lunch.

2 I'm thirsty. I'll have a glass of milk with my lunch.

3 We have a pizza for dinner on Saturdays.

4 We need a treat. We'll have a pizza tonight!

Circle the right answer.

We use *will* to talk about *instant decisions / things we do regularly.*

6 Put the words in order.

1 | to | drink | you | have | What | will |

.... ?

2 | have | a | I'll | cup | of | tea |

....

3 | he | have | to | eat | What | will |

.... ?

4 | I | have | won't | any | noodles |

....

5 | go | tomorrow | She'll | to | school |

....

6 | We | outside | won't | go | because | cold | it's |

....

7 ✏️ What will you do? Write sentences using *will* and an activity from the box below.

> study hard   stay at home   drink some water
> eat a sandwich   go to the doctor

1 I'm hungry. ....

2 I'm thirsty. ....

3 I'm sick. ....

4 I have a test. ....

5 It's raining. ....

8 Read the text and choose the best answer.

Jada: *Are you hungry, Sam?*
Sam: *A Yes, you are.*
  B Yes, he is hungry.
  C Yes, I'm starving!

1 **Ciara:** What will you have to eat?

  Sam: A I have tomato soup.

  B I'll have the tomato soup.

  C I won't have any tomatoes.

2 **Jada:** I won't have too much. I think I'll have a tuna salad.

  Ciara: A That sounds delicious!

  B I won't do it.

  C What's your favorite food, Jada?

3 **Jada:** What will you have to drink?

  Sam: A I'll have a banana and some strawberries.

  B I'll have the banana and strawberry smoothie.

  C I won't have the banana and strawberry.

4 **Jada:** I think I'll get some of the homemade lemonade.

  Sam: A Actually, I think I'll have lemonade, too. I won't have the smoothie.

  B Actually, I think I'll have lemonade, too. I will have the smoothie.

  C Actually, I think I'll have lemonade, too. I like smoothies.

5 **Ciara:** Great, are we ready to order?

  Sam: A Yes, she's great.

  B Yes, I'll wait.

  C Yes, I'll call the waiter.

6 **Jada:** This food is delicious!

  Ciara: A My sister doesn't like bananas.

  B I won't take my sister here.

  C It is! I'll bring my sister here tomorrow.

4 We could see a movie on Saturday

1 **Read the emails. When will Dan visit Lisa?**

Hi, Dan!

How are you?

I'm writing to ask you about the weekend.

What could we do on Saturday morning? We could go to the skate park or go swimming.

Also, what kind of restaurant should we go to on Saturday afternoon? There's a nice Chinese restaurant in the center of town.

I don't know what to do on Sunday. It could rain.

Let me know what you think.

Bye!

Lisa

Hi, Lisa!

Let's go to the skate park on Saturday morning. I love roller-skating.

That's a great idea about the Chinese restaurant. We could go to see a movie on Saturday evening.

We could relax on Sunday morning and go for a walk in the afternoon, if it doesn't rain.

In the evening there will be a concert at the school. We could go!

See you soon,

Dan

2 **Read and circle T (*true*) or F (*false*).**

1 On Saturday morning, they'll go swimming. T / F

2 They'll see a play on Sunday evening. T / F

3 Lisa doesn't know what to do on Sunday. T / F

4 Dan wants to relax on Sunday morning. T / F

5 They'll go to a Chinese restaurant on Saturday evening. T / F

Grammar table

It could rain.

What could we do on Saturday morning?

We could go to the Chinese restaurant.

3 **Read the text again and underline sentences with *could*.**

4 **Circle the correct answer.**

1 We *could go swimming / could swimming go* on Saturday afternoon.

2 He *could walks / could walk* in the park.

3 She *could travel / could to travel* to the United States next year if she's lucky.

4 It *could to be / could be* sunny tomorrow. We could go to the beach.

5 *Could I come / Could I coming* to your house tomorrow?

6 What *we do / could we do* on Sunday?

5 💡 Read the sentences and answer the questions.

1 We could go for a walk.

2 It could rain tomorrow.

A Which sentence is a suggestion? ....

B Which sentence is a possibility? ....

6 Put the words in order. Then write "P" for possibility or "S" for suggestion.

1 musical   see   tonight   could   a   You

.... ◯

2 morning   go   shopping   We   this   could

.... ◯

3 He   pass   could   exams   his

.... ◯

4 could   It   this   snow   winter

.... ◯

5 go   could   skating   We   tomorrow

.... ◯

6 Friday   rain   could   It   on

.... ◯

7 💬 With a friend, think about the things you could do this weekend. Fill in the table with your ideas.

	Saturday	Sunday
morning		
afternoon		
evening		

What could we do on Saturday morning?

We could go shopping or stay at home.

Shopping could be expensive. Let's stay at home.

OK, we could do some cooking!

1 Read the text. What animals can you see in the zoo?

My name is Vicky. I work at the city zoo here in Los Angeles. We have a lot of different animals from all over the world.

I like working with big animals like gorillas, giraffes, lions, and tigers. Definitely the biggest animals in the zoo are the elephants. They're the heaviest, too. The giraffes are the tallest, of course. I'd say the most dangerous animals we have here are the bears. For zoo keepers, they're more dangerous than lions and tigers. The smallest animals we have are the insects, but we have some birds that are smaller than some of our spiders!

For me the best animals are the elephants. I think they are much more beautiful and more intelligent than any other animals. They're better and funnier to watch and actually easier to clean because they love water so much. I like all our animals, so I don't think there's a "worst" animal.

2 Read and circle T (*true*) or F (*false*).

1	Vicky thinks elephants are the best animals at the zoo.	T / F
2	Lions are more dangerous than bears.	T / F
3	Vicky thinks spiders are the worst animals.	T / F
4	Giraffes are the biggest animal in the zoo.	T / F
5	Some spiders are bigger than some birds.	T / F

Grammar

Adjective	Comparative	Superlative
heavy	An elephant is heavier than a gorilla.	The elephants are the heaviest animals in the zoo.
dangerous	Bears are more dangerous than lions.	The bears are the most dangerous animals.
good	Monkeys are better at climbing than other animals.	Monkeys are the best at climbing.
bad	Bears are worse to clean than elephants.	Bears are the worst animals to clean.

3 Read the text again and underline comparative forms in blue and superlative forms in red.

13

4 Circle the correct answer.

1 Elephants are the *most heavy / heaviest* animals in the zoo.

2 Bears can be *more dangerous / the most dangerous* than other animals.

3 Giraffes are *taller / the tallest* than zebras.

4 Cleaning elephants is *more easy / easier* because they love water.

5 I think that butterflies are *more beautiful / the most beautiful* than spiders.

6 Zoo keepers think that elephants are *the most intelligent / more intelligent* animals in the zoo.

5 Read the sentences and answer the questions.

1 Elephants are bigger than bears.

2 Elephants are the biggest animals in the zoo.

3 Bears are more dangerous than elephants.

4 Bears are the most dangerous animals in the zoo.

A Which sentences compare all animals in the zoo? ....

B Which sentences compare two kinds of animals? ....

6 Complete the sentences with the correct forms of the adjectives.

nice dangerous beautiful
heavy tall small

1 Dogs are .... than cats.

2 Bears are .... animals in the zoo.

3 Giraffes are .... than elephants.

4 Elephants are .... animals in the zoo.

5 Ants are .... animals in the zoo.

6 I think butterflies are .... than snakes.

7 Draw three animals that you like. Show them to a friend. Talk about which one is bigger, heavier, the most intelligent, etc.

My cat is more dangerous than your dog!

Look, your bear is bigger than my elephant!

Your giraffe is the most beautiful animal!

A cheetah can run the fastest

1 Look at the pictures. What animals can you see? Which animal do you think is faster? Read the text to check your answer.

There are a lot of animals that can move more quickly than humans. The animal that can run the fastest is the cheetah. It runs at 120 kilometers per hour – more quickly than anything on legs.

In the sky, the bird that flies the fastest is the peregrine falcon. It can dive at about 320 kilometers per hour! That's fast!

The animal that moves the most slowly on land is the sloth, it can only travel at about 2 meters a minute!

The animal that can make the most noise is the blue whale – it sings more loudly than a jet engine.

Some people think fish are the animals that move the most quietly. They don't make much noise at all when they swim.

The animal that works the hardest is probably the bee. It never stops moving or looking for food. Maybe that's why we say someone is "as busy as a bee".

2 Read the text again and match to make sentences.

1	Bees	A	move more quietly than other animals.
2	Cheetahs	B	work harder than any other animal.
3	Sloths	C	run faster than other animals.
4	Blue whales	D	call more loudly than any other animal.
5	Fish	E	move more slowly than other animals.

Grammar

Adverb	Comparative	Superlative
fast	A cheetah can run faster than a rabbit.	A cheetah can run the fastest.
slowly	Sloths move more slowly than snails.	Sloths move the most slowly.

3 Read the text again. Underline comparative adverbs and circle superlative adverbs.

4 Circle the correct answer.

1 The peregrine falcon flies *faster / the fastest* than a cheetah runs.

2 Birds sing *quietly / more quietly* than whales.

3 Sloths move *more slowly / the most slowly* than other animals.

4 Bees work *more harder / harder* than pandas.

5 The cheetah can run *faster / the fastest*.

6 Blue whales sing *more loud / the loudest*.

5 What is different about the sentences?

1 A peregrine falcon can fly faster than a cheetah can run.

2 Cheetahs run the fastest.

3 Sloths move more slowly than tortoises.

4 The animal that moves the most slowly is the sloth.

Match to make the rules.

We add -*er* or -*est*	to adverbs that end in -*ly*.
We add *more* or *the most*	to short adverbs.

6 Complete the sentences with the correct forms of the adverbs.

1 A tortoise can run .... (fast) than a sloth.

2 A cheetah moves .... (slowly) than a peregrine falcon.

3 A cat can move

.... (quietly) than an elephant.

4 Monkeys can move

.... (gracefully) in the trees.

5 Bees work .... (hard) than any of the other animals.

6 I think a mouse can run .... (quietly).

7 Look at the list of animals. Write sentences describing how they move.

lion   shark   koala   snake   owl
bear   eagle   penguin

The penguin can swim faster than the lion.

1 The lion moves ....

....

2 ....

....

3 ....

....

8 Read the story. Choose a word from the box. Write the correct word next to numbers 1–5.

Hi, my name's Ali. Last week I went to the _____zoo_____ with my class. I wanted to see the **(1)** _____ and the turtles because they are my favorite animals. Orangutans are fast! They can climb trees very **(2)** _____ and gracefully. They jump from tree to tree and they can run on the ground. The zoo keeper told us to wait **(3)** _____ so we could see the new baby orangutan. It was very sweet!

We also saw the turtles. Turtles move more **(4)** _____ than orangutans, but maybe not in the water. We saw a big turtle – it was eating some leaves. Turtles **(5)** _____ plants, small animals, and even some fish.

I enjoyed my trip to the zoo and want to go there again with my family.

zoo	orangutans	quietly
climb	slowly	eat
whale	turtle	quickly

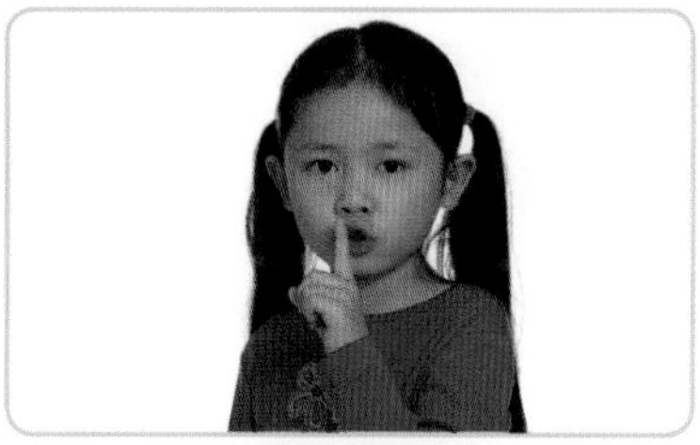

(6) Now choose the best title for the story. Check one box.

The fast orangutan ☐

Our trip to the zoo ☐

We see a turtle swimming ☐

1 Read the text. What do they think is the best? What do they think is the worst?

Fabrizio

Food
Everyone is different. Some people say pizza tastes better than pasta. They say that sushi tastes worse than French fries. I think the food that tastes the best is ice cream. What food do you think tastes the best? What food tastes the worst?

Soccer
A lot of soccer teams play well. Some people think Germany plays better than Italy. I think the best soccer team in the world is Brazil. They won the world cup four times! Which soccer team do you think plays the best? How well do you play?

Dina

Dominik

Cooking
I cook really badly. My dad says he cooks the best in our house. He cooks eggs well and he can cook pasta, too, but we all know that Mom cooks better than Dad! Who cooks the best in your house?

Smell
A lot of things can smell badly, like cheese and fish, but I think that rotten eggs smell the worst. What do you think smells the best?

Rosalina

2 Read and circle T (*true*) or F (*false*).

1 Fabrizio says that ice cream tastes better than other food. T / F

2 Rosalina says cheese smells worse than rotten eggs. T / F

3 Dominik is good at cooking. T / F

4 Fabrizio thinks sushi tastes the worst. T / F

5 Dominik's mom cooks better than his dad. T / F

6 Dina says that Brazil plays worse than Germany. T / F

Grammar

Adverb	Comparative	Superlative
well	Pizza tastes better than pasta	I think the Brazilian team plays (the) best.
badly	Sushi tastes worse than French fries.	Rotten eggs smell (the) worst.

3 Read the text again and underline comparatives in blue. Underline superlatives in red.

4 Circle the correct answer.

1 My brother thinks that sushi tastes *worst / worse* than hamburgers.

2 That green wall looks *better / the worst*! It's so ugly!

3 Germany plays soccer *better / best* than Italy.

4 I like cooking. My mom says I cook *better / best* in the family.

5 Sam is a good student. He speaks English the *best / worst* in our class.

6 I hate seafood. It smells *the worst / worse*.

5 Read the sentences and answer the questions.

1 I think that pizza tastes better than soup.

2 I think rice tastes the worst.

3 I think that pizza tastes best.

4 I think that rice tastes worse than pizza.

A Which sentences compare two things? ....

B Which sentences talk about one thing? ....

6 Underline the mistakes and correct the sentences.

1 He's a good tennis player. He plays the better in the school.

....

2 My sister cooks badly than me. She burns everything.

....

3 I think that Chinese food tastes best than Italian food.

....

4 I did the better on the math test yesterday. I got the lowest grade.

....

5 I like getting up early. I work worst in the morning.

....

6 Juana plays the violin well than me. She's very talented.

....

7 ⬤ **Can you do these activities better than a friend? Discuss with your friend.**

play soccer   cook   speak English   sing   write   spell   dance

How well do you play soccer?

I think I play better than you.

Yes, I play worse than you.
But I speak English better than you!

8 📄 **Read the text. Choose the right words and write them on the lines.**

OUR HOBBIES

Hello! My name is Beatriz and this is my brother, Hugo. We both love soccer! Hugo can play very _____*well*_____ but I play **(1)** _____ than my brother. I scored the most goals in school! We do other sports, too. I play baseball and Hugo can run very fast.

We're not good at everything. We swim very **(2)** _____ . Next week we will start swimming lessons because we want to be the **(3)** _____ !

We like cooking, too. I cook **(4)** _____ than Hugo. His favorite food is chocolate and I like Japanese food. Hugo doesn't like fish and I hate spinach. It tastes the **(5)** _____ !

	good	*well*	*best*
1	better	well	the best
2	bad	badly	worst
3	worst	better	best
4	worse	well	badly
5	badly	worst	worse

1 Read the text. Where can you see these signs?

Hi, I'm Emre and I'm with my best friend, Lucy. We live in a small town called Winston.

Today we're walking around our town. We're taking pictures for a school project on rules. We're looking for signs that tell us what to do or what not to do.

I saw the No Entry sign on the street. It means you can't go into that area!

The Staff Only sign was in a coffee shop. Customers mustn't go in that room.

The No Talking sign was on the wall in the quiet part of the library. It means you mustn't talk. Shhh!

We saw the Do Not Disturb sign in a hotel.

The Danger sign was outside a factory. It means you must be careful!

Lucy saw the No Cell Phones sign in the movie theater. You mustn't use your phone when you watch a movie.

We saw the No Texting While Driving sign by the road. We think that's a really good rule! You can't text when you're driving because it's dangerous.

There are so many rules!

2 Read and write T (*true*) or F (*false*).

1 There's a factory in Emre's hometown. ....

2 You must be quiet in some parts of the library. ....

3 They saw the No Entry sign on the street. ....

4 You must use your phone at the movie theater. ....

5 It isn't dangerous to text while driving. ....

Grammar

I/You/He/She/It must stay out of this building.	I/You/He/She/It mustn't/can't go in there.
We/You/They must wear a helmet.	We/You/They mustn't/can't run there.

3 Read the text again and underline sentences with *must*, *can't*, and *mustn't*.

4 Circle the correct answer.

1 You *must / mustn't* wear a helmet at the skate park.

2 Drivers *must / can't* use their cell phone while driving.

3 Customers *must / mustn't* go through the Staff Only door.

4 You *must / mustn't* be home at 6 p.m.

5 You *must / can't* talk in some parts of the library.

6 We *can't / must* run here! The floor is wet.

5 Read the sentences and answer the questions.

1 You mustn't talk.

2 You must be careful.

3 You can't skateboard here.

A Which sentences tell you not to do something? ....

B Which sentence tells you to do something? ....

C What form of the verb comes after *must*?

   verb with *to* / verb with *-ing* / verb without *to* or *-ing*

6 Put the words in order.

1 library You mustn't at the talk loudly

....

2 skate park wear a helmet at the You must

....

3 go into You that area can't

....

4 careful must be You

....

5 can't You that door go through

....

7 Write rules for the swimming pool using some of the activities in the box below.

> run   ~~wear a swim cap~~   listen to the instructor
> shower before entering pool   push anyone   bring your own towel

You must wear a swim cap.

1 ....

2 ....

3 ....

8   **Look, read, and write.**

You must turn off your <u>phone</u> .
What must you leave in the cloakroom? <u>your suitcase</u>

Complete the sentences.

1 In the museum you can't eat or ....

2 You mustn't take pictures with your ....

Answer the questions.

3 Where must you put your trash? ....

4 What can't you bring into the museum? ....

Now write two sentences about the rules.

5 ....

6 ....

9 What do you need to do?

1 **Read the text. What chores does Ivan do?**

My name is Ivan. That's me! I'm vacuuming. It's Saturday morning. My parents and I do our chores on Saturdays.

We all have different jobs. First, I have to make my bed. Then I have to clean my room. After that, I have to vacuum the living room. My mom doesn't need to help me. My dad has to mop the floor and do the dishes. He needs to take out the trash, too. We get really tired. I'm glad that I don't have to do chores every day.

After we finish, we need to rest. We need to have a drink and something to eat. My mom makes us lunch and we always have a big cake for dessert. She needs to rest, too, after all that cooking! Then we don't need to do any more chores for the rest of the day.

When do you have to do your chores?

2 **Read the text again and match to make sentences.**

1	We have to do our chores	A	after I finish my chores.
2	I need to rest	B	help me.
3	First, I have to	C	on Saturday morning.
4	My mom doesn't need to	D	make my bed.

3 **Read the text again. Underline a question with *have to*, a positive sentence with *has to*, and a negative sentence with *need to*.**

4 **Circle the correct answer.**

1 My dad *has to / have to* mop the kitchen floor.

2 On weekends we *don't has to / don't have to* go to school.

3 My mom *have to / needs to* work in the morning.

4 The students in my class *has to / have to* work hard.

5 Do you *need to / needs to* do chores in your house?

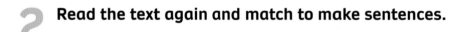

Grammar

I/You/We/They have/need to tidy my room.	I/You/We/They don't have/need to go to school on Sundays.
He/She/It has/needs to do chores on Monday.	He/She/It doesn't have/need to mop the floor.
Do you have to clean the floor?	Yes, I do. No, I don't.
When do you have to do your chores?	
What chores do you need to do?	

24

5 🔦 Read the sentences and complete the rules.

1 I have to do my homework.
2 He has to do his chores.
3 We don't have to go to school.
4 She doesn't need to cook.

We use *has* with .... and *have* with ....

We add .... or .... to make negative sentences.

6 Put the words in order.

1 has   his   bed   to   make   He

....

2 I   don't   do   to   have   dishes   the

....

3 has   to   My   sister   her   homework   do

....

4 I   early   wake   up   need   to   for   school

....

5 have   to   from   the   walk   home   swimming   pool   We

....

6 you   to   need   Do   do   your   today   chores

.... ?

7 💬 Ask two friends what they *have to* and *need to* do. Put a check or a cross in the table.

Name	1	2 ....
get up early		
walk to school		
wear a school uniform		
eat school lunch		
do your homework		

Do you have to walk to school?

No, I don't. I can ride my bike.

Do you need to do your homework?

Yes, I do. I need to do my homework every night.

1 **Read the text. Who has a birthday on the last day?**

I'm James. This summer my family's going to Florida for a vacation and I'm very excited. There's so much to see. My mom planned everything already. We aren't driving or going on a train – we're flying!

We're staying in a hotel in a big park called Ocean World. There's an aquarium with a water park next door and a big amusement park behind it.

In the first few days, we're visiting the aquarium and watching some of the animal shows. There are sharks, dolphins, and turtles at the

aquarium. In the evenings, there's a big fireworks show in the park. We're watching it on the first night.

On the weekend, we're visiting the water park. I'll ride the Super Drop. It's one of the biggest slides in the world! I'm really excited.

On the last day, it's my brother's birthday. He'll be 12 and he's having a party at a big restaurant. I don't think we'll want to come home.

What are you doing on your vacation this year?

2 **Read and circle T (*true*) or F (*false*).**

1 James will see sharks and dolphins. T / F

2 James is excited because he's riding a big water slide. T / F

3 The family is staying in an amusement park. T / F

4 James's brother is having a birthday party at the aquarium. T / F

5 James's family is going on a vacation to Florida. T / F

6 They're watching a fireworks show on the first night. T / F

Grammar

I'm riding the Super Drop.	I'm not riding the Super Drop.
He/She/It's coming to my party.	He/She/It isn't coming to my party.
We/You/They're visiting the aquarium.	We/You/They aren't visiting the aquarium.
Are you leaving on Sunday?	Yes, I am. No, I'm not.

3 **Read the text again and underline verbs ending with *-ing*.**

4 Circle the correct answer.

1 *We're staying / We stay* at a hotel this summer.

2 Tomorrow, *I'm visiting / I visiting* my grandmother.

3 *I'm leaving / I left* next Monday.

4 *He has / He's having* a party next week.

5 *They had / They're having* a class meeting tomorrow morning.

6 We *aren't doing / isn't doing* homework tonight. We're playing soccer.

5 When is this happening? Read the sentences and match.

1 I'm having a party tomorrow.

2 I'm having a party right now.

3 I'm having a party.

A At the moment.

B In the future.

C Can be at the moment or in the future.

6 Complete the sentences with the correct forms of the verbs.

have   come   not go   take
visit   meet

1 We .... an exam tomorrow.

2 I .... my uncle next week.

3 She .... to the library on Friday.

4 .... your friend at the park tomorrow?

5 I .... a party at my house next week.

6 He .... to my house tomorrow morning.

7 What are you doing this weekend? Plan your activities.

~~go to school~~   do homework
go to the skate park   go swimming
go to the bowling alley   relax at home
go to the movie theater
visit my grandparents   go shopping

	morning	afternoon	evening
Friday	go to school		
Saturday			
Sunday			

I'm going to school on Friday morning.

1 .... in the afternoon.

2 ....

3 ....

4 ....

5 ....

8 Read the text and choose the best answer.

Chen: *Hi, Selen, what are you doing?*
Selen: (A) *I'm packing for my trip.*
      B *She's busy.*
      C *I'm not going.*

1 **Chen:** When are you going on your trip?
    Selen: A I'm busy tomorrow.
          B Saturday sounds nice.
          C I'm going next week.

2 **Chen:** Where are you going?
    Selen: A I'm going to check.
          B I'm visiting an amusement park.
          C I visit an amusement park.

3 **Chen:** What will you do there?
    Selen: A I see a lot of rides and a pirate ship.
          B I'll ride a pirate ship and drive a bumper car.
          C I'm ride a bumper car and drive a pirate ship.

4 **Chen:** Where are you having lunch?
    Selen: A We're having lunch next to the lake.
          B We have lunch next to the lake.
          C I'm hungry!

5 **Chen:** What are you doing after lunch?
    Selen: A We ride a pirate ship.
          B Tomato soup and chicken.
          C We're watching a show at the theater.

6 **Chen:** When are you coming back?
    Selen: A We go there next weekend.
          B We're flying back next Sunday.
          C I'm visiting my grandma next week.

1 Look and read. Write the correct letter next to each comment.

Hi everyone! I have to do a project about interesting places. What are the best places to visit in your country? What could I do there?
Thanks,
Claudia

1 ....

Dear Claudia,

You could write about Angkor Wat. It's the biggest temple in the world and it's more than 900 years old. You could take a bicycle tour there. It goes through the temple. It's amazing!

2 ....

Hi, Claudia!

For me, London is the best city in the world. You could visit many great restaurants and the most famous stores, like Harrods! You have to go to Camden Market. You mustn't forget to visit Big Ben or go on a London bus!

3 ....

Claudia,

The most beautiful place in the world is the Great Barrier Reef. You have to go there. It's so amazing! You could go swimming and see the most wonderful fish. But you mustn't stand on the reef – you could break it.

2 Read the text again and match to make sentences.

1 At the Great Barrier Reef, Claudia could

2 In London, Claudia could

3 In Angkor Wat, Claudia could

4 Claudia mustn't

5 Claudia would like

A go to many famous stores.

B go swimming.

C some help and advice.

D take a bicycle tour.

E stand on the Great Barrier Reef.

3 Read the text again. Underline a sentence with *have to*, a sentence with *mustn't*, and a question with *could*.

4 Circle the correct answer.

1 We're late for school. You *need to / could* walk faster!

2 You *mustn't / must* do your homework for tomorrow.

3 What would you like to do tonight? We *could / must* go to the movie theater.

4 We *mustn't / must* talk during the exam. We have to be quiet.

5 She has English tomorrow. She *needs to / could* take her English book to school.

6 Do you like Mexican food? We *couldn't / could* order some tacos.

29

5 Complete the sentences with the correct forms of the adjectives.

1 You must go to school. It's .... (important) than watching TV.

2 I like your soccer team. It's .... (good) than mine.

3 We could go to the theater. It's .... (exciting) than the park.

4 You must try it. It's .... (good) food in the world.

5 English is .... (easy) than Chinese.

6 We have to visit Russia. It's .... (large) country in the world.

6 Underline the mistakes and correct the sentences.

1 Tyler is the better friend I have.

....

2 She must to go to work.

....

3 Do you have much chores to do tonight?

....

4 I need go shopping with my mom.

....

5 I must forget my sister's birthday.

....

6 Tokyo is most expensive than Lima.

....

7 What is the best place to visit in your country? Write a response to Claudia's post. Suggest some activities she could do there.

●●●

Hi, Claudia!

The best place to visit in my country is...

....

....

....

....

8 Read the text and choose the best answer.

Angela: Hi, Paul. Where are you going?

Paul: (A) I'm going home. I need to catch the bus.

B I'm going home. I mustn't catch the bus.

C I'm going home. I could catch the bus.

1 **Angela:** Can you come to my house tonight?

Paul: A Sorry, I have to do my homework.

B Sorry, I could do my homework.

C Sorry, I mustn't do my homework.

2 **Angela:** How about tomorrow?

Paul: A I have to clean my room.

B I mustn't vacuum the kitchen.

C They need to learn English.

3 **Angela:** What are you doing on Sunday afternoon?

Paul: A We must meet.

B I have to go.

C Not much. We could meet in the afternoon.

4 **Angela:** What could we do?

Paul: A We mustn't meet.

B We could go to the movie theater.

C We need to go to school.

5 **Angela:** OK, what time?

Paul: A I need to meet you at two.

B I must meet you at two.

C We could meet at two.

6 **Angela:** Great, see you on Sunday.

Paul: A Bye, I see you.

B Bye, see you!

C Bye, I could see you on Sunday.

1 **Read the text. When did people begin writing?**

Writing

A long time after people started talking, they started writing. Historians think that people began writing more than 5,000 years ago!

The ball point pen

Before people started using ball point pens, they had to fill pens up with ink every time they wanted to write! A Hungarian man called László Bíró made the ball point pen in 1943. Pilots could use the pens when they were high in the air and people could use them when they were outside in bad weather.

The typewriter

The first modern typewriters came from the United States. You could use them to type letters. You could find a typewriter in every office and every school in the world! After people started using computers, typewriters became less popular.

The text message

Text messages are much more recent than you think. A Finnish engineer called Makkonen sent the first message in 1992. He thought they would be useful for business. People could quickly send short messages from their cell phones. He didn't know how popular and useful text messages would become!

2 **Read and write the name of the invention.**

1   People could use this when they were outside in the rain.

   ....

2   This is a short message you could send quickly.

   ....

3   People used this in offices to type letters.

   ....

4   It became less popular after computers were invented.

   ....

3 **Read the text again and underline sentences with _when_, _before_, and _after_.**

Grammar

When they were high in the air, pilots could use ball point pens.

Pilots could use ball point pens when they were high in the air.

Before people started using ball point pens, they had to fill pens up with ink.

People had to fill pens up with ink before they started using ball point pens.

After people started using computers, typewriters became less popular.

Typewriters became less popular after people started using computers.

People could send messages from their cell phones.

4 Circle the correct answer.

1 When he was young, my grandpa *before / when / could* ride a horse very well.

2 I did my homework *when / before / after* I went to bed. Now I don't have to do it tomorrow.

3 *When / Before / After* people started using typewriters and computers, they used pens to write.

4 She speaks Spanish *when / before / after* she's in Spanish class.

5 People started writing a long time *when / before / after* they started talking.

6 He *when / could / after* read when he was five.

5 Which activity happened first? Match.

1 I had a drink before I went to school.

2 I had a drink when I was at at school.

3 I had a drink after I finished school.

A Both activities happened at the same time.

B I had a drink first.

C I finished school first.

6 Complete the sentences.

> could (×2)   After   when (×2)
> before

1 When I was seven years old, I .... play the piano.

2 I am always polite .... I visit my grandmother.

3 .... László Bíró invented the ball point pen, you didn't need much ink to write.

4 You need to do a lot of work .... you take the test.

5 Pilots could use ball point pens .... they were flying.

6 My brother .... play the guitar when he was six years old.

7 Choose one activity from each column to make sentences.

come to school	go to sleep
watch TV	do homework
have dinner	read
see friends	have a cookie
be six years old	leave school
be in preschool	ride a bike

1 ....

before ....

2 ....

after ....

3 When .... ,

I could ....

8 **Read the text. Choose the right words and write them on the lines.**

CALCULATORS

People started using calculators ____*when*____ they went on sale in the 1960s. **(1)** _____ calculators, people usually used a pen and paper to do math. Thanks to calculators they **(2)** _____ add and subtract large numbers more easily.

Students can make calculations more quickly **(3)** _____ they use a calculator. You can't always use a calculator **(4)** _____ you're taking a math test, but you can use it to check your calculations **(5)** _____ the exam.

	when	*could*	*before*
1	When	Before	Could
2	when	before	could
3	could	when	before
4	after	before	when
5	after	when	before

1 **Read the text. Was Tammy busy last weekend?**

Hi, Tammy. What were you doing on Saturday morning?
Like all Saturday mornings, I was walking in the park with my sister and our dog.

In the afternoon, there was a concert at our school, but I wasn't watching the concert. I was playing it! I play the drums and I was part of the band. It was fantastic.

What were you doing on Saturday night?
I was eating pizza in a restaurant with my family. It was really good. It was a surprise for my sister's birthday.

What were you doing at eleven o'clock on Sunday morning?
I was doing my chores. For most of the morning, I was washing the dishes and cleaning my room. I wasn't doing my homework.

Were you doing your homework on Sunday afternoon at three o'clock?
No. We went to the skating rink, but we weren't skating. We were watching a hockey game. Our team won.

I was doing my homework that evening. Then I watched a movie with my family.

2 **Read and write *Yes* or *No*.**

1 I was playing a concert on Sunday. ....
2 I was doing my homework on Sunday. ....
3 I was walking in the park with my sister on Saturday. ....
4 I was doing my chores on Sunday. ....
5 I was eating pizza on Saturday night. ....

Grammar

I **was playing** the music!	I **wasn't listening** to music.
We/You **were bowling**.	We/You **weren't sleeping**.
Were you **visiting** your grandparents?	Yes, I **was**. No, I **wasn't**.
What **were** you **doing** on Sunday morning?	

3 **Read the text again and underline *was/were* + *-ing*.**

4 **Circle the correct answer.**

1 Ella *was doing / was do* her homework until eight o'clock last night.

2 You *are sleeping / were sleeping* on Sunday morning.

3 I *wasn't / weren't* watching soccer last night. I was playing on a soccer team.

4 You were watching a movie last night. You *weren't to do / weren't doing* your chores.

5 *Was / Were* you shopping yesterday morning?

5 **Read the sentences and circle the right answer.**

Was is the past form of *have / are / am*.

Were is the past form of *are / is / go*.

6 **Complete the sentences with the correct forms of the verbs.**

We ___weren't speaking___ (✘ speak) Spanish in French class.

1 At nine o'clock this morning, I _____ (✔ have) my breakfast.

2 I was sick yesterday so I _____ (✘ play) basketball.

3 Can I have my pen? You _____ (✔ use) it this morning.

4 What _____ you _____ (do) last night?

5 You _____ (✘ listen) to the teacher. Now you don't know what the homework is.

7 **Write what you were doing in the table. Then ask and answer questions with a friend.**

Time	Me	....
seven o'clock this morning		
on Sunday at four o'clock		
last night at eight o'clock		
one hour ago		
on Saturday night		

What were you doing at seven o'clock this morning?

I was sleeping.

8   Read the text and choose the best answer.

Daisy: *What were you doing on Sunday morning?*

Alyssa: *A   We weren't in the living room.*

        Ⓑ   *We were cleaning the living room.*

        C   We are walking in the park.

1   **Daisy:**   Were you helping your parents?

    Alyssa: A   Yes, I need help.

        B   Yes, my parents were there.

        C   Yes, I was.

2   **Daisy:**   What were you doing?

    Alyssa: A   I was putting away my toys.

        B   I always do that.

        C   No, we weren't.

Sunday morning

3   **Daisy:**   Were you dusting, too?

    Alyssa: A   Yes, I was watching TV.

        B   No, I'm not dusting.

        C   No, I wasn't.

4   **Daisy:**   Were you watching TV on Sunday afternoon?

    Alyssa: A   Yes, it was Sunday.

        B   No, it wasn't on TV.

        C   No, we weren't.

Sunday afternoon

5   **Daisy:**   What were you doing?

    Alyssa: A   We are cleaning the kitchen.

        B   We were cleaning the kitchen.

        C   We don't clean the kitchen.

6   **Daisy:**   You work too much! What were you doing Sunday evening?

    Alyssa: A   We were watching a movie at the movie theater.

        B   We weren't there on Sunday.

        C   We were eating breakfast.

1 **Read the story. Who helped the lion?**

One day a lion was sleeping in the jungle. He was enjoying the cool wind and dreaming of lunch. A little mouse ran out of the bushes and bumped into his nose. The lion woke and caught the mouse under one of his paws. He smiled because he wasn't expecting his lunch so soon.

"Please don't hurt me," cried the mouse. "I can help you if you let me go."

The lion thought it was funny so he let the mouse go.

A few days later, men were hunting in the jungle. They weren't trying to kill animals. They wanted to take them to the zoo. They trapped the lion in a net.

The same mouse was walking through the forest when he heard the lion's roar. At once he ran to the sound. He saw the lion trapped under the net and saw that he was struggling to get out.

"I can help," said the mouse and he started to bite at one of the ropes of the net. Soon, the lion was free.

No kindness is ever a waste!

2 **Match the questions to the answers.**

1   Who trapped the lion?

2   Why did the lion let the mouse go free?

3   How did the mouse help the lion get free?

4   What was the lion doing after he was trapped?

5   What was the lion doing at the beginning?

A   He bit through the ropes.

B   He was sleeping.

C   He thought the mouse was funny.

D   He was roaring.

E   Hunters from the zoo.

Grammar

He/She/It was sleeping in the forest.	He/She/It wasn't eating.
They were hunting.	They weren't trying to kill the animals.
Were they catching the animals?	Yes, they were. No, they weren't.
What was the lion doing?	

3 **Read the story again and underline positive sentences with _-ing_ in blue and negative sentences with _-ing_ in red.**

4 Circle the correct answer.

1 A moose *was walking / walking* through the forest.

2 Leon *wasn't feel / wasn't feeling* very hungry.

3 Was *she playing / playing she* soccer yesterday evening?

4 My mom and dad *weren't working / was working* last Saturday.

5 My siblings *was study / were studying* at school yesterday, like me!

5 What is different about the sentences?

1 He was dreaming of something nice.   2 He wasn't playing the piano.

3 They were walking in the jungle.   4 They weren't watching TV.

Match to make the rules.

| We use *was/wasn't* with | they. |
| We use *were/weren't* with | he, she, and it. |

6 Put the words in order.

1 your   last   doing   What   cousin   was   night

.... ?

2 last   night   My   mom   was   working   late

....

3 to   the   rabbit   They   catch   were   trying

....

4 doing   What   was   at   five   Dawid   o'clock

.... ?

5 her   wasn't   eating   dinner   She   family   with

....

7 Remember the story called *The Hare and the Tortoise*. Write the story. Answer the questions to help you.

1 Who was slow and who was fast?   2 What did they decide to do?

3 Who was running faster?   4 What did the hare do?

5 What was the tortoise doing?   6 Who won the race?

8 Look at the pictures and read the story. Write some words to complete the sentences about the story. You can use 1, 2, or 3 words.

One afternoon, Maria was walking home from school and she decided to visit her grandma. It was a beautiful day and her grandmother was working in the garden. She was picking fruit and putting it in a big basket.

Maria's grandma gave her a basket full of fruit. There were three bananas, two guavas, and a big mango.

Maria __was walking__ *home from school.*

1   Maria's grandma _____ fruit from her garden.

2   Grandmother _____ Maria a basket of fruit to take home.

Maria started to walk home. After a few minutes, she was feeling tired so she decided to carry the basket on her head. It was easier to carry it this way. A monkey was watching her from a tree. It saw the bananas and swung down. When Maria wasn't looking, it reached out and took the bananas.

3   Maria put the basket on her head because she _____ .

4   A monkey _____ bananas in the basket.

5   When Maria _____ , the monkey stole the fruit.

Soon, two green parrots were flying over her head. They looked down and saw the juicy guavas in Maria's basket. Quietly, they flew down and picked up the guavas in their claws. All the time, Maria was walking happily home. A few minutes later, Maria was walking along a stone wall. A crow was sitting on the wall. When Maria was walking by, the crow picked up the mango in its beak and flew away.

When Maria got home she looked at her basket. It was empty!

6   Two green parrots _____ in the sky.

7   The crow stole Maria's mango when she _____ a wall.

1 Read the text. Who has a lot of accidents?

I'm Daniel and I live with my mom, dad, and my little sister, Jane. She's 9 years old and she has a lot of accidents… almost every day!

On Sunday, she was running in the hall when she fell. She knocked over a vase and it broke. My mom was really angry. Jane was very sorry.

On Monday, she was looking for something in our dad's office when she spilled his coffee all over his papers. He wasn't happy!

On Tuesday, she was riding her bike to school when she fell off onto the grass. She wasn't looking where she was going. She was wearing a helmet, so she was OK.

On Wednesday, she kicked a ball over the fence while we were playing soccer in the yard. I looked for it but I couldn't find it. I loved that ball! She was really sorry.

She lost her pen on Thursday. She said she lost it while she was studying in the library. She needs to go and look for it! I'll help her.

It's Friday. I wonder what she'll do today…

2 Read and circle T (*true*) or F (*false*).

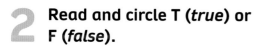

1   Jane was studying in the library when she lost her bag.   T / F

2   She was wearing a helmet while she was riding her bike.   T / F

3   Jane knocked over a vase while she was running.   T / F

4   She spilled her milk while she was eating lunch.   T / F

5   We were playing soccer when she kicked a ball over the fence.   T / F

Grammar

She was running in the hall when she knocked over the vase.

She didn't spill her milk while we were eating breakfast.

He hurt himself because he wasn't wearing a helmet.

What was he doing when you saw him?

3 Read the text again. Underline sentences in which one action happened while another action was happening.

4 **Match to make sentences.**

1 I was having my breakfast when   A I was playing soccer.
2 It started raining   B I spilled my drink.
3 She walked into a wall   C because she wasn't paying attention.
4 I scored a goal while   D while they were playing outside.

5 **Read the sentence and answer the questions.**

I was riding my bike when I fell off.

A Which activity happened for a longer time? ....

B Which activity interrupted the longer activity? ....

6 **Complete the sentences with the correct forms of the verbs.**

1 She .... (have) lunch when she .... (spill) her drink.
2 We .... (run) on the field when we .... (fall) over.
3 My phone .... (ring) while I .... (watch) a movie.
4 I .... (not play) soccer when Natalie .... (arrive).

7 **Imagine you had a very unlucky day. Write what happened to you.**

go to school / start raining

I was going to school when it started raining ....

1 play basketball / fall over

....

2 ride my bike / ride into a puddle

....

3 spill my drink / eat my lunch

....

4 lose my wallet / do the shopping

....

5 walk into a lamp post / use my cell phone

....

6 make a sandwich / cut my finger

....

8 Imagine you arrived at a park. Look, read, and write what the people were doing.

Grandpa was sitting on __the bench__ .

Where was the little boy? __next to his mom__

Complete the sentences.

1 The girl jumping rope was wearing a ....

2 The boy in a green T-shirt was ....

Answer the questions.

3 What was the man in a blue sweater doing? ....

4 Was the old man sitting on a bench? ....

Now write two sentences about the picture.

5 ....

6 ....

There was nothing to do

1 **Read the text. Who was in the painting?**

Last year my family went on a vacation. We stayed in a big, lonely house in a dark forest.

My parents liked it because everything was quiet. My brother and I didn't like it there. There was nothing to do. It was too cold to go out and it was a long way from the nearest town. There was nowhere to go.

At night the house was cold and full of shadows. At the top of the stairs was a painting of a rich old man. My mother told me that he was someone important and perhaps he was the owner of the house. I was staying with my brother upstairs in the bedroom and my parents were next door. In the middle of the night, we heard something banging. It came from somewhere downstairs. It was loud.

"Maybe it's the old man in the painting," said my brother. "Maybe he's looking for something… or someone!"

My brother and I went down the stairs to the kitchen. When we opened the door, we saw that the window was open. It was banging in the wind. There was no one there at all!

2 **Read and write *Yes* or *No*.**

1   There was someone in
    the kitchen.   ....

2   At night they heard something
    banging.   ....

3   The children liked the house.   ....

4   There was nothing for the
    children to do.   ....

5   The children went down to
    the kitchen.   ....

3 **Read the text again and circle words beginning with *some-*, *no-*, or *every-*.**

Grammar

There was nothing to do.

No one knew who he was.

There was nowhere to go.

We heard something banging.

He was someone important.

It came from somewhere upstairs.

My dad liked it because everything was quiet.

Everyone likes going to the beach.

It was cold and dark everywhere.

4 Read and match the sentences.

1   I was bored.   A   I want someone to help me.

2   I'm hungry.   B   I need something to eat.

3   I can't do my homework.   C   I had nothing to do.

4   We have a ball.   D   We need somewhere to play basketball.

5 Complete the rules with the missing words.

┌─────────────────────────────┐
│ things   people   places   │
└─────────────────────────────┘

We use *everyone*, *someone*, and *no one* with ....

We use *everything*, *something*, and *nothing* with ....

We use *everywhere*, *somewhere*, and *nowhere* with ....

6 Underline the mistakes and correct the sentences.

1   You can ask everything to help you.

    ....

2   I'm thirsty, can I have someone to drink?

    .... ?

3   This place is boring, there's everywhere to go!

    .... !

4   Something likes Sonia. She's very friendly and funny.

    ....

5   You feel lonely when you have everyone to talk to.

    ....

6   Somewhere is knocking on the door. Can you open it?

    .... ?

7 Write a spooky story. Answer the questions to help you.
Make sure you use words that start with *some-*, *every-*, or *no-*.

1   Where did you go?   2   Who did you go with?

3   What was the place like?   4   How did you feel?

5   What did you see?

1 **Read the messages. What sport are Sam and Jacob doing?**

Dear Sam,

I'm so excited that you are visiting this weekend.

Are you going to take the bus? What time are you going to arrive on Saturday morning? We can pick you up from the bus station.

The karate competition is starting at twelve o'clock. I think we're going to do well in the competition. I can't wait!

In the evening we're going to go to the movie theater. What movies do you like?

Bye,

Jacob

Hi, Jacob!

I'm excited about the competition, but I have bad news. I fell on Monday and I hurt my arm. I'm not going to take part in the competition. I'm still going to watch and help you!

I'm not going to take the bus. My mom will drive me to your house. We're going to arrive at about eleven o'clock. Then my mom will pick me up from your house at eight o'clock in the evening.

I like karate movies. Can we see one?

See you on Saturday,

Sam

2 **Who are the sentences about? Write J (*Jacob*), S (*Sam*), or B (*both*).**

1 I'm going to arrive at eleven o'clock. ....

2 I'm going to take part in the karate competition. ....

3 I'm excited about the karate competition. ....

4 I'm going to the movie theater. ....

Grammar

I'm going to arrive at 11:00.	I'm not going to drive.
We/You're going to take the train.	We/You aren't going to take the bus.
Are you going to watch a movie?	Yes, we are. No, we aren't.
What are you going to do tonight?	

3 **Read the messages again and underline sentences with *going to*.**

4 Circle the correct answer.

1 It's too cold to go outside today, I *am going / am not going* to go for a walk.

2 I'm really excited, I'm *going to / not going* go to Belgium next year.

3 What *are you / you are* going to do this weekend?

4 We need new shoes. We *are to / are going to* go shopping tomorrow.

5 Please hurry up, you *are going to / am going* be late.

5 Read the sentences and circle the right answer.

1 I'm going to see a movie tomorrow night.

2 I'm not going to go to school today.

We use *be going to* + verb to talk about *things happening now / future plans / things which happened before*.

6 Put the words in order.

1 I'm   watch   going   a   movie   to

....

2 school   go   not   to   to   I'm   today   going

....

3 catch   We   to   bus   aren't   the   going

....

4 to   ice-skating   going   this   Are   go   weekend   you

.... ?

5 not   to   English   I'm   speak   going

....

7 Someone gave you $5,000 and you have to spend it all this weekend. What are you going to do?

*I'm going to go shopping.
I'm going to buy a new laptop!*

*I'm going to go to Disneyland on Saturday!
Then, on Sunday, I'm going to...*

8 **Read the text. Choose the right words and write them on the lines.**

SHADOW THEATER

This weekend we _____are_____ going to do a shadow theater at our school and I'm going to act in it. It's called Aladdin. It's on Saturday night at seven o'clock.

I'm going to **(1)** _____ very busy, but I'm **(2)** _____ going to do any homework and I'm not going to do any chores!

I am going to **(3)** _____ a great time. My family is coming and so are all my friends and relatives. I have a ticket for you, too! You **(4)** _____ going to sit at the back. You're going to sit at the front!

When the show ends, we're going **(5)** _____ come to a party at my friend's house.

	am	*are*	*is*
1	am	to be	be
2	isn't	not	no
3	have	having	to have
4	are	isn't	aren't
5	to	on	for

1 **Read the article. What will Antoine do in Times Square?**

Do you think being a young millionaire is easy? Next week, Antoine Moreau is going to visit New York. It's his first visit to the city and he's going to be very busy. He isn't going to have a relaxing time.

Everywhere he goes people are going to talk to him. Are the journalists going to leave him alone? No, they aren't! They're going to follow him everywhere.

He's going to stay at one of the best hotels in the city, the Ritz in the main square. On Saturday night, he's going to go to the movie theater in Times Square to see a movie premiere. Many famous people and journalists are going to be there.

The next day, he's going to wake up early. He's going to open a new shopping mall on Wall Street in the morning. In the afternoon, he's going to visit the Central Park Wildlife Center. In the evening, he has more to do. He's going to watch the famous basketball team the New York Knicks play against the Chicago Bulls.

2 **Read and answer the questions.**

1 Where is Antoine going to stay in New York?

2 What is he going to do on Saturday night?

3 Where is he going to go on Sunday morning?

4 What is he going to watch on Sunday evening?

Grammar

He/She/It's going to be busy.	He/She/It isn't going to be quiet.
People are going to talk to him.	They aren't going to leave him alone.
Is he going to go to the theater?	Yes, he is. No, he isn't.
What are they going to do?	

3 **Read the article again and underline one question and one negative sentence with _going to_.**

4 Circle the correct answer.

1 They *is going to / are going to* go to the aquarium.

2 *Are they going / Is they going* to go to the swimming pool?

3 They *aren't going / 're going not* to visit the museum.

4 *Is going to she / Is she going to* travel tomorrow?

5 Draw a line between the columns to connect the forms.

Long form	Short form positive	Short form negative
1 he is	it's	he isn't
2 she is	they're	it isn't
3 it is	she's	she isn't
4 they are	he's	they aren't

6 Complete the sentences.

is going to   isn't going   They're going   are going to   going

1 My sister _____ to go to the party tonight. She's sick.

2 Xavier _____ go to the soccer stadium next week.

3 _____ to watch hockey tomorrow night.

4 Is your brother _____ to visit the museum next week?

5 My friends _____ visit me next week. I'm so excited!

7 Look at the table and circle the activity they are going to do. Then tell your friend.

Family member	What do they have?	What are they going to do?
Grandpa	a tennis racket	play tennis / go shopping
Mom and Dad	cups of tea	ride bikes / drink some tea
Sister	plane tickets	do her homework / fly to Paris
Cousins Joe and Ali	winter jackets	make a snowman / play the guitar

What's your grandpa going to do?

He has a tennis racket. He's going to play tennis. He isn't going to go shopping!

8 Read the text and choose the best answer.

László: *Hi, Andrej. What are you going to do on Sunday?*

Andrej: Ⓐ *I'm going to go to a skateboard competition.*

     B *I'm not going to eat that.*

     C *I'm going to the park on Saturday.*

1 **László:** What time are you going to wake up?

    Andrej: A I'm not going to have a busy day.

        B I'm going to wake up at about 8:00.

        C I'm going to have breakfast.

2 **László:** Who's going to go with you?

    Andrej: A I'm not going to go shopping on Sunday.

        B My coach is going to go with me.

        C I'm with my family.

3 **László:** What's your coach going to do?

    Andrej: A He's catching the train.

        B He visited the museum.

        C He's going to help me warm up.

4 **László:** Are your parents going to watch?

    Andrej: A Yes, I have a new watch.

        B My parents are doctors.

        C Nothey aren't. But my friends are going to be there!

5 **László:** Are they going to cheer for you?

    Andrej: A Yes, they are.

        B Yes, they are nice.

        C Yes, we're all going.

6 **László:** Are you going to win?

    Andrej: A Yes, I'm going there.

        B I hope so!

        C No, he isn't.

19 He won because he trained hard

1 **Read the text. How old was Usain Bolt when he became a professional athlete?**

Usain Bolt is one of the fastest people on earth and they call him "Lightning". Bolt was born in Jamaica in 1986. He loved sports and always played a lot of cricket and soccer, but his teachers said he was better at running. At the age of twelve, he was the fastest runner in the school. His father said he was fast because he ate a lot of potatoes!

He won a lot of competitions at school and when he was fifteen, he went to the World Athletics Championships in Kingston, Jamaica. He won the 200 meter race in a record time.

When he was eighteen, Bolt became a professional athlete so he could focus on running. He wanted to be the best.

In 2005, he went to the World Championships in Helsinki, Finland. He got into the finals, but he finished last! Then, at the Beijing Olympic Games in 2008, he won a gold medal in the 100 meters in a record time of 9.89 seconds.

At the Rio Olympics in Brazil, Bolt won gold in the 100 meters again! He has eight Olympic gold medals, but there may be more to come!

2 **Read and circle T (*true*) or F (*false*).**

1   Bolt was better at soccer than running.   T / F

2   His father said that eating potatoes made him fast.   T / F

3   Bolt has six Olympic gold medals.   T / F

4   He came in last place in the finals at the World Championships in Helsinki.   T / F

5   Bolt won the 200 meters at the World Athletics Championships.   T / F

6   Usain Bolt is sometimes called "Lightning".   T / F

Grammar

She did gymnastics and she was good at it.

You won the gold medal because you trained hard.

They trained hard so they won the gold medal.

They trained hard, but they didn't win the gold medal.

3 **Read the text again and underline sentences with *and*, *because*, *so*, and *but*.**

4 **Match to make sentences.**

1 I went to the store,

2 We won the soccer game

3 She didn't study very hard

4 I ran the fastest

5 They went to the Olympics

6 We were really happy

A so she failed her exam.

B so I won the race.

C and won three gold medals.

D but it was closed.

E because we scored more goals.

F because we won three gold medals.

5 **Read the sentences and complete the rules with *and*, *but*, *because*, or *so*.**

1 I like lemonade and I like coffee.

2 I like lemonade, but I don't like coffee.

3 I ate a banana because I was hungry.

4 I was hungry so I ate a banana.

We use _____ to show the result of an action.

We use _____ to show the reason for an action.

We use _____ to give additional information.

We use _____ to say that something is different or is a contrast.

6 **Complete the sentences with *and*, *but*, *so*, or *because*.**

1 I passed all my exams _____ I made my parents proud.

2 My brother is the best student in the school _____ he studies a lot.

3 On Thursday evenings we go swimming _____ then watch a movie.

4 I'm learning English _____ I want to speak to people around the world.

5 I want to speak to people all over the world _____ I'm learning English.

6 He is very fast, _____ he didn't win the race.

7 **Finish the sentences with your own ideas. Then, share your answers with a friend.**

1 I like going to school because _____ .

2 I like my house, but _____ .

3 On Saturday I _____ and _____ .

4 I didn't do my homework because _____ .

5 It was my birthday last week so _____ .

6 My dad is really nice, but _____ .

1 **Read the text. What jobs are mentioned?**

A dangerous job

Firefighters are people who are often in real danger. They go into buildings and forests which are on fire. They risk their lives! You have to be someone who is brave to be a firefighter.

A horrible job

I think dentists have horrible jobs. They look at mouths that smell and they pull out teeth that are rotten. I wouldn't like to be a dentist. Would you?

A quiet job

Librarians have quiet jobs. They work in libraries and there isn't much noise there. They help people that need information. I think they need to be people who love books, too!

An exciting job

If you are someone who likes excitement, then you could be a police officer. They do different things every day and try to catch people who break the law.

An interesting job

Doctors have very interesting jobs. They meet people who have a lot of different problems. They also need to know all about bodies and diseases. You have to be someone that is really intelligent to be a doctor.

2 **Read the text again and match to make sentences.**

1. Librarians are people who
2. Police officers try to
3. Dentists are people who
4. Firefighters are people who
5. Doctors are often people who

A. catch people who break the law.
B. risk their lives to help others.
C. pull out rotten teeth.
D. are intelligent and caring.
E. love quiet places and books.

Grammar

Firefighters are people **who** are often in danger.

Librarians help people **that** need information.

They go into buildings and forests **which** are on fire.

Dentists look at mouths **that** smell.

---

3 **Read the text again. Underline sentences with _who_ in red, _which_ in green, and _that_ in blue.**

4 Circle the correct answer.

1 Teachers are people *who / which* like working with young people.

2 The United States is one of the countries *that / who* I want to visit.

3 A taxi driver is usually someone *who / which* can drive well.

4 This is the key *which / who* opens the door.

5 We're looking for someone *that / which* can cook well.

6 I like animals *who / which* have soft fur.

5 Read the sentences and complete the rules with *who*, *which*, or *that*.

1 He's someone who likes soccer.

2 This is the laptop which keeps breaking.

3 He's the man that lives next door.

4 I love the book that I got from my brother.

We use _____ with people.

We use _____ with things.

We use _____ with people and things.

6 Complete the sentences with *who*, *which*, or *that*.

1 The boy _____ lives next door is my best friend.

2 Did you find the book _____ you were looking for?

3 She's the girl _____ sits next to me in class.

4 That's the activity _____ we have to do for homework.

5 I need someone _____ I can trust.

6 My mom likes movies _____ make her cry.

7 Choose a person or thing from the box below. Take turns describing and guessing.

> pizza   ice-skating   turtle   my mom   fireworks   vacuum
> cleaner   cheetah   police officer   shark   karate

It's something that lives in the sea and eats fish.

It's a shark! My turn. It's someone who...

1 Read the story. What did Sam and Jack do when they saw the bear?

Sam and Jack were hiking through the forest together. It was getting dark, so Sam became worried.

"I'm afraid of bears," said Sam.

"Don't be scared," said Jack, "I'm good at fighting bears. I've fought many of them before. Nothing is going to hurt us!"

A few minutes later, they heard something move behind them. It was a big brown bear. When Jack saw the animal, he quickly climbed up a tree. Sam tried to climb up, too, but he couldn't. Jack didn't help him, because he wanted to make sure he was safe first. He climbed higher up the tree.

Sam laid down under the tree because it was too late to run. When the bear came over to him, it sniffed his ear. Sam held his breath so the bear thought he was dead. Soon enough, the bear decided to leave Sam and went back into the dark forest.

After the bear left, Jack climbed down from the tree. He looked very afraid.

"What did the bear say to you?" asked Jack. "I saw him whisper in your ear."

"He said I shouldn't be friends with someone who tells lies," said Sam.

2 Read the text again and match to make sentences.

1 Sam was angry with Jack

2 Sam laid down

3 It was getting dark

4 Jack climbed up a tree

5 Sam didn't breathe

A because it was too late to run.

B so the bear thought he was dead.

C when he saw the bear.

D because he lied to him.

E so Sam became scared.

3 Read the story again. Underline sentences with *and*, *so*, *but*, and *because* in red. Underline sentences with *after* and *when* in green.

4 Circle the correct answer.

1 They were walking through the forest *when* / *but* they saw the bear.

2 I was scared of the dog *after* / *so* I ran away.

3 He asked his friend to help, *but* / *so* she didn't want to.

4 She went to bed *after* / *because* she was tired.

5 *After* / *So* I did my homework, I watched TV.

6 My brother plays baseball *and* / *but* he's very good at it.

5 Read and choose the correct answer.

1. **Mom:** Hi, honey, what did you do at school today?

   Vera: A Something! It was boring.

   B Nothing! It was boring.

2. **Mom:** Oh… Where did you go at lunch time?

   Vera: A Nowhere, we stayed inside.

   B Nothing, we stayed inside.

3. **Mom:** What did you eat?

   Vera: A I bought everyone from the cafeteria.

   B I bought something from the cafeteria.

4. **Mom:** What did you learn today? Anything interesting?

   Vera: A We did a project about nothing in China.

   B We did a project about somewhere in China.

5. **Mom:** Who did you walk home with?

   Vera: A Someone from my class.

   B Everything from my class.

6. **Mom:** What are you going to do tomorrow?

   Vera: A I don't know. I hope it's something better than today.

   B I don't know. I hope it's everyone better than today.

6 Underline the mistakes and correct the sentences.

1. There's everything to do here. I'm bored!

   ....

   ....

2. He sat in the yard so the sun was shining.

   ....

   ....

3. So my dad washed his car, he cooked dinner.

   ....

   ....

4. I want to talk to people on my trip to New York when I'm learning English.

   ....

   ....

5. I like my country so I don't like the weather.

   ....

   ....

6. There's somewhere behind you!

   ....

   ....

7 Use conjunctions to connect the phrases and write a story. You can add some information to make the story more interesting.

get out   go hiking   fall into a hole
~~be bored~~   try to climb out
see a wooden chest
bring the treasure to the museum
~~call a friend~~   go get help
walk in the forest   be in a cave
open the chest   look around

One Saturday morning I was bored so I called a friend…

8 Look at the pictures and read the story. Write some words to complete the sentences about the story. You can use 1, 2, or 3 words.

Hi! I'm Vicky. This is a picture from my sister's wedding last year. It was a really great day and the weather was nice. In the morning, we all got up very early to get ready on time. After breakfast, a hairdresser came to our house to do our hair. My sister was nervous about the wedding. I was nervous, too.

Vicky had a great day at her sister's .....wedding..... .

Vicky woke up early .....because..... *she had to get ready.*

1 .... they had breakfast, a hairdresser came to do their hair.

2 Vicky's sister was nervous .... getting married.

At eleven o'clock, a big limousine came to pick us all up and take us to the church. When we arrived, all our family and friends were already there. My sister looked very beautiful. My mom was very happy, but she didn't cry! After the wedding, a photographer took pictures of everyone.

3 All the family and friends were at the church .... they got there.

4 Vicky's sister looked beautiful .... their mom was very happy.

5 The photographer took pictures ....

We had the reception party at a big hotel. My sister and her new husband, Tom, sat at a big table in front of everyone. Before the meal, Dad and Tom made speeches. Tom's speech was really funny. After the meal, we had a big cake. Then there was a party and we danced until one o'clock in the morning. It was a fantastic day.

6 .... they arrived at the hotel, Vicky's dad gave a speech.

7 They had a meal .... the party.

1 **Read the interviews. Did the students have a good week?**

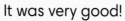

Hi, Amy. How are you?
I'm fine, thanks!

Did you have homework this week?
Yes, but not too much. I could still practice the piano after school.

Which day was the best this week?
I enjoyed Thursday the best this week – we were painting pictures and listening to music. It was cool.

What are you doing tonight?
I think I'll watch TV with my family.

What are you going to do this weekend?
I'm going to go bowling on Saturday morning. On Sunday afternoon I'm watching a musical at the theater but I need to do my chores on Sunday morning.

Hi, Lucas. Did you have a good week?
It was very good!

What were you studying at school this week?
We were doing math problems this week. They were hard.

Which class was the worst this week?
Music. No one likes music!

How many times did you play baseball this week?
I played twice after school.

What are you doing this evening?
I don't know. I could visit my friend or I could watch a movie with my brother.

What are you going to do this weekend, Lucas?
I'm going to baseball practice on Saturday. After that I'm going to go to a water park with my friends.

2 **Read and circle T (*true*) or F (*false*).**

1 On Saturday Lucas is going to watch a movie.   T / F
2 The day that Amy enjoyed the most was Sunday.   T / F
3 Amy did some homework this week.   T / F
4 Amy's going to watch TV with her friends tonight.   T / F
5 Lucas was doing math problems at school this week.   T / F

3 **Read the interviews again and underline questions about the past in blue and questions about the future in yellow.**

4 Match the questions to the answers.

1 What are you doing tonight?

2 What are you going to do this weekend?

3 What were you doing in class this week?

4 What were you doing last night?

A I'm going to go to the aquarium on Sunday.

B I was watching some fireworks.

C I'm doing my homework before I go bed.

D We were studying history.

5 Complete the sentences with the correct forms of the verbs.

read   help   visit   not listen   ring   can

1 My grandpa _____ speak five languages when he was young.

2 A vet is a person who _____ sick animals.

3 I'm sorry, I _____ . Could you please repeat?

4 My cousin _____ us next week.

5 I _____ a book when the phone _____ .

6 Put the words in order.

1 going   What   weekend   are   you   do   this   to

_____ ?

2 are   going   on   Where   vacation   you

_____ ?

3 have   What   to   will   drink   you

_____ ?

4 many   did   times   tennis   How   play   they

_____ ?

5 you   last   What   doing   night   were

_____ ?

7 Prepare an interview. Choose six questions from this unit, then ask and answer with a friend. Write down the answers.

8 Read the story. Choose a word from the box. Write the correct word next to numbers 1–5.

Hello, my name's Lucy. This week was my first week at a new
_____*school*_____ . It was a bit **(1)** _____ , but not bad. I was
(2) _____ because I didn't know anyone. Everyone was very
(3) _____ so I felt OK. The school is very big and there
are a lot of classrooms. When I **(4)** _____ for the restroom,
I got lost and I didn't know where to go! Yesterday we **(5)** _____
about the United States. It's a really good school and the teachers are
great. I think I will really enjoy coming here.

school	worried	were playing
friendly	difficult	was looking
were learning	was finding	were running

(6) Now choose the best title for the story. Check one box.

Lucy's good week ⬚

Lucy's first week ⬚

Lucy's bad week ⬚

Irregular Verbs List

Infinitive	Past Simple
be	was/were
begin	began
blow	blew
break	broke
bring	brought
buy	bought
build	built
can	could
choose	chose
come	came
cost	cost
cut	cut
do	did
draw	drew
drink	drank
drive	drove
eat	ate
fall	fell
feel	felt
fight	fought
find	found
fly	flew
get	got
give	gave
go	went
grow	grew
have	had
hear	heard
hold	held
keep	kept
know	knew
lay	laid
leave	left

Infinitive	Past Simple
lead	led
let	let
lie	lay
lose	lost
make	made
mean	meant
meet	met
pay	paid
put	put
read	read
ring	rang
run	ran
say	said
see	saw
sell	sold
send	sent
set	set
sing	sang
sit	sat
sleep	slept
speak	spoke
spend	spent
stand	stood
take	took
teach	taught
tell	told
think	thought
understand	understood
wake	woke
wear	wore
win	won
write	wrote

Pearson Education Limited

KAO Two
KAO Park
Harlow
Essex
CM17 9NA
England
and Associated Companies throughout the world.

www.English.com

First published 2019
Fourth impression 2020

ISBN: 978-1-292-21958-5

Set in Daytona Pro Primary 12/16pt

Printed and bound in China (GCC/04)

Acknowledgements

The publisher would like to thank the following for their kind permission to reproduce their photographs:

(Key: b-bottom; c-centre; l-left; r-right; t-top)

123RF.com: 21cl, 21cr (top), 23bl, 23bc, 23br, 44 (main), 59l, 61c, dolgachov 61tr, gbh007 6, 11, Iakov Filimonov 24, Jit Lim 17tc, marosbauer 17br, robertmandel 17cr, stockbroker 8; **Alamy Stock Photo:** ZUMA Press, Inc. 52t; **Datacraft Co Ltd:** 61br; **Pearson Education Ltd:** Jon Barlow 51, Gareth Boden 18br, Jörg Carstensen 61tl, Handan Erek 46r, Pearson Education, Inc. 37t, 37b, Arvind Singh Negi / Red Reef Design Studio. Pearson India Education Services Pvt. Ltd 40, Ratan Mani Banerjee. Pearson India Education Services Pvt. Ltd 43, Jules Selmes 18tl, 18tr, 18bl; **Shutterstock.com:** 1968137 21br, 23 (top & centre), Aga Es 17tl, Antonio Abrignani 44 (inset), Arcady 21cr (bottom), Arnoud Quanjer 15b, artincamera 29 (A), Artisticco 28, astudio 21tr, AVAVA 61cl, Blend Images 10, BMJ 56t, Chris Hill 15t, Dariush M 13t, David Mckee 17cl, Dmitri Ma 4, Eric Limon 58b, espies 59r, Ethan Daniels 17bl, Galyna Andrushko 56b, Ingrid Prats 26b, Jarno Gonzalez Zarraonandia 48, John Panella 58c, K. Jensen 38, Konstantin Chagin 61bl, Leremy 54, Lucian Coman 46l, Luciano Mortula 29 (B), michaeljung 20, Michele Cozzolino 61tc, Mila Supinskaya 13b, Monkey Business Images 35, moshimochi 41, obkung 17bc, Oleksiy Mark 34, oliveromg 58t, Peerayot 32, Pressmaster 31, RimDream 49t, Ryan Carter 26t, Samot 29 (C), Solovyova Lyudmyla 17c, StacieStauffSmith Photos 21bl, Stephen Coburn 21tl, SurangaSL 49b, szefei 61bc, Thomas M Perkins 17tr, xc 52b, yalayama 61cr

All other images © Pearson Education

Cover photo © **Getty Images:** DigitalVision